Clockworks

Rajesh Kumar Gouda

"To the ones I used to look up to
And the ones I'm still learning to become."

Foreword

When he told me he's writing a poetry book, I
thought, "Of course you are." It just made sense.
These poems feel like conversations we've had—late
at night, during long walks, or when things didn't
quite make sense.
There's nothing fancy here, and that's the best part.
It's honest, it's quiet, and it stays with you. Some
poems made me think about things I hadn't thought
about in a while. Others just felt comforting, like
someone saying, "Yeah, I get it."

This book is him, through and through. And I'm
really glad it's out in the world now.

Raj Kumar Gouda

Preface

This book began as scattered thoughts—written late at night, between lectures, during walks, and in quiet corners of rooms I thought I had outgrown.
At first, it was just a way to understand myself. Then it became a way to speak when I didn't know how to. Each poem is a timestamp, a preserved breath. They aren't polished confessions, but they are honest.

You'll find pieces of childhood games, moments that bruised quietly, rooms that remembered more than people did, and a slow kind of healing—so slow, it felt like standing still.
But the stillness spoke too.

If you're holding this, I hope you find a version of yourself in here. One that needed a whisper, not a shout.

This is not a manual for becoming whole.
It's just a hand reaching out.

A library of one

There's nothing much in my room,
a bed, a mirror, and a once-empty shelf.
Is it made of neem?
or sheesham?
I couldn't care less.
The only thing this old, greasy shelf harbours
is over the corner, a phantom book.

Did someone buy this for me?
Or did I pick it up from a street?
I once asked these to myself,
and now it's just...
there, dusty and still,
as if the past got tired of screaming
and the future is annoyed for what's yet to come.

Was it there when I was six? Yes;
Is it still here when I'm twenty-two? It is.
Back then I couldn't reach it.
And now, it won't open to me.
But it's not printed,
I can feel it
it's a bit more personal and I feel it.

Years later, it opened up for me.
The imprints were quite similar and,
the writing matches up with my own.
Duly dated pages with proper guides,
some frustrated scribbles and
some vague text that I don't know of.

The book is alive and it scares me a bit,
It adds up pages on its own.
Pages that caught fire on random nights
and some were drenched in tears?
Some had potatoes for whatever reason or
had moths squeezed between them.

None of it made sense!
so I left it where it was,
At the greasy top right corner
of a shelf made up of teak.
So I could gaze at it from my bed,
and... it could watch over me at night?

[1st October, 2024 — 09:55 PM]

Timestamps

"Some memories don't fade; they simply fold themselves into quieter corners of us."

[4th October, 2023 — 10:27 PM]

I was ten, I was scared.
Biting a painted nail would yell out,
"There's a monster underneath my bed".
Mum, used to hold me,
Close!
She would tell me, to befriend him
but I was too afraid to hear her out.
So I ignored it! ran away from it!
And came so far, maybe too far.
Now I'm twenty-one,
laying silent on my bed
drooling a leg to the side,
Waiting! No, hoping
for the monster to drag me out of here.
But he won't,
the monster underneath is long gone
and so does the boy with a painted nail.
…
And yet I'm still scared.

Fading Footprints

Sometimes I doubt
of being a prisoner of my other self.
Faded, confused, empty
and strapped to these rusty shells.
Strapped to myself
who scratches my selcouth dreams,
unreasonable, unbearable, unspeakable
and immovable are my schemes.
My schemes being simple —
no triumph, no fall,
just a stillness
too loud to crawl.
It's foolish to search for meaning
in hollows you cannot touch.
Some days, the silence fits;
Most days, it bruises much.

Maybe that's the lesson —
not every locked door awaits a key;
sometimes, you notice the walls
because you stayed too long to see.

Prisoner

Sometimes, it cries out —
his heart, that is.
Clenching his teeth,
he leaves, expressionless.
Amidst bleak and dull lights,
he wanders the dusky corridor,
To find a soul or a ghost,
just to get those eyes cold.

The moon has heard his cries,
the night has seen him cry,
but the day would lie to us.
To keep secrets among themselves.
He is tired but won't say anything,
he is afraid but won't tell anyone,
So he's quiet with some words,
unspoken & unheard.

Unspoken

[27th November, 2023 — 09:12 AM]

The piano used to sing.
Now, it's more of a hum.
A buzz, like a thousand tiny legs
scrambling under the surface,
lost between the keys,
filling the empty spaces.

I thought I heard music,
but now I only hear
the sound of something
trying to find its way
through a melody that's not quite right.

Each note is a tiny tremor,
a broken echo of what once was,
a distant whisper that
never reaches the ears.

The ants are inside,
moving from one string to the next,
working in silence,
their tiny bodies
like fragments of forgotten thoughts.

They make their homes
in the cracks no one notices
until the air feels wrong,
too thick with things left unsaid.

I keep playing,
hoping the notes will align, but they never do.
They bend under the weight of something hidden.
I hear them now — the ants —
louder than the music.

Their movement in the dark
fills the silence between the keys
until everything feels too loud and
too small at the same time.

I wonder if I'll ever find the sound
that used to fill the space or if
I'll always be listening
for something that's already gone.

Ants in the Piano

[23rd December, 2023 — 12:05 PM]

It was supposed to save me. The rope.
I kept it coiled,
neatly by the window ledge like faith.
A silent promise that if it came to it,
there would be a way down.

But one day, I found it tangled—
not by wind, not by time,
but by hands
that might have been mine.
I don't remember the knotting, only the result.

The knots were clever.
Elegant, even.
Each one a memory twisted tight,
a refusal to forget
disguised as survival.

I tried to untie them.
Gently, then desperately.
But pulling only tightened things,
like the rope resented being
touched after all this time.

There's a knot with the name
I never said.
Another with the letter
I never burned.
One smells faintly of a hospital corridor.

Now, I just stare.
I trace them some nights, fingertip to loop,
wondering if unravelling means
to remember.

Some nights,
I count the knots instead of stars.
They're steadier.
They don't vanish when I blink.

And in the morning,
I hang the rope back exactly where it was.
Like a promise
I'm still trying to believe in.

Knots

[7th February, 2024 — 10:07 AM]

This morning,
a red thread curled itself
around my wrist again—
thin, bright,
too deliberate to be an accident.
It didn't start there, just ended there,
looping itself as if
it knew I'd notice.

I tugged it.
Of course I did.
What else is one to
do with a thread
that keeps appearing
where skin meets cloth?

It caught beneath the hem,
threaded through
yesterday's silence
and the day before.
It stitched itself into
the sleeve of every apology
I never wore properly.

It has no end, only length.
Each pull tightens
the fabric beneath my skin,
makes the world feel
half a size too small.

Some days, I pretend it's a reminder—
a mark of something unfinished, important,
like the string on a finger
meant to remember
something I keep forgetting
on purpose.

Other days, it just feels like
anger that learned to sew.
I don't know who holds the spool,
but I've stopped pretending it's me,
and I've started wearing longer sleeves.

Red threads on my sleeves

[18th February, 2024 — 00:40 AM]

The books on my shelf are all incomplete.
Some letters missing—
always the same ones.
Silent among the others, nestled between pages
that whisper of something lost.

They were never there, not really.
I thought I felt them once,
a familiar weight,
but now,
they're just a shape I can't trace.

It's the kind of thing you can't point to,
but it haunts your mouth when you try to speak.
A word that doesn't exist—
missing its curves,
its marks that would make it whole.

They're not just any letters,
not just any sounds.
They're the ones that would've
made the difference,
that could've named the space.

I'm stuck.
They would've told me who I was
before I lost the meaning.
I keep rearranging them,
the letters, over and over,
like building a story from pieces that don't fit.

Sometimes, I forget— forget the gap.
But then I see it in the silence,
in how everything I say
feels incomplete.

And when no one's around,
I trace the edges of the missing ones,
wondering if they're still there—
in the things I can't name,
the things that have no words
but still make their presence known.

'U' and 'I'

[8th March, 2024 — 07:25 PM]

The moths came first,
silver scraps stitched by the dark,
drifting in and out
of the golden hue's tired breath.

A lamp coughs above,
sending ripples
over bruised pavements,
over my scraped knees,
over the marble half-lost in my hands.

One circled once —
twice —
then vanished in a crackle,
as if the night itself had blinked
and yet none stopped.

They didn't flinch just kept dancing—
wings brushing
against the brittle light,
seeking something in there,
their small bodies couldn't be named.

14

I thought they were laughing,
the way they darted and crashed,
wings spilling powdery breath
into the evening air.

Some clung to the glass,
others simply fell, quiet as breath.
I learned —
even a broken glow
could ask them of everything.

So I stepped forward,
into the hum of the streetlight.
The moths spun their last
and the night folded itself around me.

Moths

It's Cold!
Not like those warm winter nights,
those Christmas's merry ice
but Cold! Dead, Quite, Cold!
I could feel those shivers
of little leaflets covered in dew,
burdened with me and my words,
trying and failing yet again.
There's nothing above,
stars, comets, wishes... nothing.
All I could see is ashes
left when the fire grows cold!
I hear some lively murmurs
"Isn't the moon beautiful!" They talked.
"Why can I not see it?"
"When will I share a night,
the same as them?" I whispered to no-one.

"Yet another moonless night for me... "

Shivers

[7th June, 2024 — 02:10 AM]

To you, under the sunlight.

The seasons ahead are a little tangled, but don't rush to
pull at the knots. Some things are meant to stay messy for
a while, like laces you never learned to tie properly, like
songs you forgot halfway through but kept singing anyway.

There's a boy who makes the dust dance when he runs
ahead of you. He laughs like nothing in the world could
ever touch him. He will teach you how to scrape your
knees and wear the bruises like badges, how to outrun
shadows without looking back. Hold on to those
afternoons.
They are smaller than you think, but they will glow in the
corners of your memory when the rooms get colder.

One day, he will falter.

You might not notice at first—the way his laughter starts
catching on sharp edges, the way he stares too long at the
ground.
When it happens, don't run ahead without him. Wait. Wait
even when it feels foolish.
He will need you to remember him louder than he
remembers himself.

If the road splits, take the quieter turn—the one where the trees lean a little heavier and the wind knows your name. It won't look the right way. But not every right way is loud, and not every wrong way is broken.

When you feel the weight of too many unopened doors, sit down. Trace the cracks in the sidewalk. Name the colours of the sky until they change. They always do, even when you're not watching.

And if someday, you forget how to find your way back, look for the blue sun you once drew in crayon.
It was never a mistake. It was a map. Somewhere far ahead, someone is still learning to run through the rain because of you.

Stay a little longer under the sunlight.
Stay a little longer in yourself.

In all the ways that matter.
Me.

Letter No. 2

[8th June, 2024 — 05:15 AM]

And soon,
I'll simmer down,
left behind in the turmoil,
like a cigarette crushed
beneath someone else's leather.
Getting cold,
turning subtle,
becoming nothing but ashes.

I won't stand —
I don't wish to.
Tired of trying, and for whom should I?
Too much for some,
too little for others.
Forgive me,
you beings who can think,
for I was too stubborn —
even for myself.

Ember

"Healing doesn't come all at once — sometimes it begins with a quiet 'I'm here.'"

I never thought I would be the kind
to carve someone's name into the walls,
to build mornings out of memory,
to want someone tucked
into every tomorrow.

But she moved through like light,
slipping under a locked door,
sieving through closed curtains —
quiet, steady, and patient.

The dust won't settle somehow,
and the long-shut windows
hum again.
The fingers don't tremble anymore,
and the tongue
doesn't bleed on words.

I don't know what you dream about
when you close your eyes,
but in the small, secret corners
I only dream of this:

a forgotten garden, still water,
ashes I never thought would cool —
a fire that keeps burning.
Selfishly...
I hope it never goes out.

Still burning

We were together under dim lights,
shivering through those frosty nights.
Slipping out to catch a glimpse of her,
talking for hours, as time grew blur.

Those distant meetings on my rooftop —
she would blush; the drapes would drop.
I spoke of things I never do —
things I love, and things I rue.

I spent evenings chasing her,
and slept through nights gazing at her.
But should I confess how I feel?
How do I do it — should I kneel?

At midnight, the lights turned amber,
a rose in hand, in late December.
Through the chilling winter dew,
it's the moon I've been talking to.

Confession

I sat beside her,
as the afternoon folded
into soft gold,
and the world pressed against the glass,
and waited.

She held the paper like
one would cradle a fledgling —
gentle, uncertain, fragile.

I had written a hundred things before:
notes, forgotten lines on napkins,
but never a letter.

A letter —
something meant to travel the sky,
carrying a piece of my breath inside it.

A letter is not just ink,
it is a river,
built with trembling hands,
hoping to find the one shore
brave enough to answer.

It wasn't about perfect words,
but those perfect pauses,
the spaces
where your heart almost speaks,
then hesitates.

Letters are stitched with silences,
anchored by the weight of unsaid things,
sent into the air like birds,
too wild to ever truly return.

The pen felt different then —
not a tool, but an offering.
I did not write that day,
just sat there,
a name waiting at the tip of a wave.

To You…

Perfect pause

Does the sky feel sorrow,
or is it the way she smiles?
Tears drip onto the leaflets,
and the Earth readies for a date.
Fragrance swirls in between,
but the winds might be late.
The clouds grow anxious,
bored — the sun setting down.
The birds carry messages
of him, somewhere around.
When misty dew came to rest,
The sun was the witness, so was the moon.
He gifted a million stars as jewels —
she wasn't ready for what transpired soon.

Holding her hands at the horizon,
elegant, yet way too juvenile,
he asked,
"Are you feeling sad?
Or is it the way you smile?"

The Sky and the Earth

[28th February, 2023 — 08:50 PM]

To you, in search of flowers.

She makes things look easy — like catching sunlight in her hands, like tying words into small, careful bundles. You watch and wonder how it comes so naturally to her, the way she folds feelings into sentences, the way her laughter fits perfectly into the spaces between silence.

Maybe you are still clumsy at it.
Your letters stumble. Your words get too heavy sometimes, too shy other times. But you are trying. You are trying in the only ways you know how.

Maybe you could write her something today — even if it's just a line or two. Maybe you could tell her how her presence feels like sitting by a window you didn't know was open, how the dust looks golden when she's around. Maybe you could tell her she made the paper seem less empty.

"Hey,
Should I speak to you or to myself?
When your arm wraps around mine,
when we hug and hold still for a moment,
I feel different. I feel special.

28

I've been rude — I apologize.
I've been late — and I regret it.
But somehow, you make me tranquil
when your head rests on mine.

I admit — the sunset was lovely,
and the moon's beauty never lies,
but I've found something softer,
something lovelier —
in your cajole-coated eyes.

We didn't say much that day,
but our silent stares filled my blanks.
Two steps to the right, two steps to the left —
they spoke everything I had wanted to say:
that I've accepted you as..."

You wonder sometimes if it's enough —
if the letters will ever carry the weight of what you're
feeling, or if they will always fall short, like bridges that
don't quite reach the other side.
You wonder if you should write more, do more and be
more.

Maybe tomorrow, you could find a prettier piece of paper.
Maybe you could learn how to draw the small flowers she
likes.

Maybe you could ask her what her favourite word is, and
write it again and again until it feels like your own.
You are still learning.
But you are learning because she made it seem worth
trying.

That must count for something.

Still clumsy as you are.
Me.

Letter No. 1

I'll call you,
when fear sits heavy on my chest,
when I'm beaten but still moving through.
so you can remind me —
that it's alright to lean,
that your shoulders are still mine to borrow.
Because you are the one
who has seen me cry and seen me shy,
seen me brave and seen me break.

I'll call you,
when happiness finds me,
so we can hold it together.
and when sadness finds you,
so you won't have
to hold it alone.
Because you are someone,
because —
You are my person of choice.

Minerva

Lately things have been different
have I changed with time?
Things that mattered once
are irrelevant now.
Things that haunted me
are dusted in my rusted memories.
I am afraid,
if I'll be able to remember you,
remember the days,
which feels like yesterday.
If I'll be able to reimagine that sky,
who was the witness,
to two little kid's oaths.
A promise, we made that night,
underneath the saffron painted leaves,
with our tranquil fingers intertwined,
that someday,

We'd run along with those comets,
and will seek that other half of the moon.
Together.

Promise

Somewhere in your silence,
I lose my voice too.
As if you're waiting
for someone else
to hear you.

Your smile falls softly,
like leaves,
but I don't know—
If they're in autumn
or in spring?

You once spoke of forever,
Now you speak
of the weather.
And I wonder —
who holds your promises now.

You breathe,
but it feels like drowning.
You laugh,
but it tastes of goodbye.

And here I am,
still curious —

Can I still be the one
you'd turn to?
still asking —

Are you curious about me?

Curiosity

I used to whisper to the moon,
thinking it was you —
soft, far, and just there.
I swear, I thought the lights were mine —
a flicker stitched into my bones,
quiet, but certain.

But I was wrong.

The moon — a mere reflection,
and you, my sun...
burning, bold, and bright.
Was it ever me at all?
Or just you, slipping through my cracks,
making me beautiful?

I don't know who I am,
or what do I look like
when you look away from me.
I can hear myself hollow again —
dragged through the dark hours,
and forgotten by the skies.

Is it love or longing?

Stitched into my skin,
making me tilt and encircle you,
and calling it my own?
Is it fine to be your ghost light,
or am I just an ashen moon?

Ashen moon

[4th August, 2023 — 10:15 PM]

I thought I was loving her,
but I was only filling the spaces in me,
trying to drink from a well
that was never mine to empty.
I mistook her hands for anchors,
her voice for a cure,
her presence for permission
to forget myself.

I kept reaching—
for light, for warmth, for forgiveness—
never asking
how much she had left to offer.

I thought my hunger was beautiful.
Thought wanting her was enough.
But love isn't hunger — love is seeing.
And I never really saw her, did I?
When her hands shook
from carrying us both,
when her silences stretched longer than her laughter,
I stood there — stupid with emptiness,
watching her walk away.

I did not chase her. Maybe I knew:
I was never there — to run.
Now the hollow places inside me
echo louder, all of them wearing her name.

This wasn't love.
It was hunger, dressed up in poetry,
and it cost me the only thing
that ever made me want to be better.
Sometimes,
I wonder how long she carried me
before she realized
I would never be enough
for both of us.

Hunger

"We were told to move forward, but nobody warned us how heavy our own shadows could be."

[16th June, 2024 — 06:47 PM]

I… remember a strange kid,
sitting down the street
under the solitary lamp.
Legs crossed in torn shorts,
bathing under and over
the flickering shade.

Cheery for those tiny moths,
who kept dancing and swirling
around that holy fire and
in awe of that golden globe,
which shone
under the drizzle of cries,
as if a spirit wants to be burned.

Last lights goes off and
it's not just him,
but the blanket of stars
and a bed of green
as if it's his home.
Zooms out and it's just him,
stranded amidst the 'good night' murmurs
from the people next door.

With dawn the lamp shattered,
the moths burned and
a little cold body was taken back home.
I wonder what I chose that night
"to be a moth? or
to be a street light?"

Street Light

The door stands ajar,
just wide enough to let
the dust creep in,
a slow invasion—
it crawls like old memories,
coating the air in silence,
layering the room with forgotten time.

A shadow of a touch,
a whispered creak,
but no one enters.
The door holds its breath,
waiting for a knock
that will never come,
for footsteps that will never fall—
It frames a monument to absence.

The room rots from within,
its corners heavy
with things undone.
It decays in silence,
weighed down by broken promises.

The floor, a graveyard of dreams
that never had a chance
to take flight.
The door, forever open,
exposes nothing but emptiness.

A threshold untouched,
a promise dissolved into the thin air—
...and the dust,
heavy with forgotten time,
smothers what remains.

A gap in air

[1ˢᵗ July, 2024 — 02:18 AM]

The room whispers to me,
as if it remembers more than I do;
the curtains keep waving "hey"
at the windowsill, hoping—just once—
that I'll wave back.

The table is cluttered
with nothing but
a forgotten cup of coffee and some blank papers,
their corners curled—
flinching or maybe hiding from me.

I've been here too long,
watching the air stiffen
with unspoken words.
and hoping the flickering lamp
might hallucinate me into something better.

The pen wobbles down
on my unsteady fingers,
trying to scribble
some unknown words.

But it leaks—quiet and slow,
not enough to stain the room,
but just enough to
ruin the margins.

Yet, the room exhaled softly,
finally giving in.
Maybe the words were out of shape
or too large against this silence.

But flowers that I pressed in between
will have to speak for me.

The room spoke first

[7th July, 2024 — 04:52 AM]

I don't turn on the lights—
It's too soothing, too gentle a lie
when the darkness holds me like this.
It knows me,
more than the light ever could.

It creeps in quiet, like old friends,
twisting into shapes that should not exist.
Longer arms, sharper teeth
made from the corners of my mind,
from the things I've tried to forget.

They wait with patience,
like monsters reaching for each other,
to hold me, to pull me under.
They move an inch closer with every blink,
shift shapes with every breath I take.

I lie still, but the bed crawls beneath me—
insects, tiny things that scurry and crawl,
their legs whispering across my skin.
I don't move, not because of fear,
but because every movement invites them closer.

Now I'm familiar with them.
They're not just shadows anymore—
they are everything I've ever lost,
every fear that's slithered beneath my skin,
every thought I've tried to bury in the dark.

I don't turn on the lights—
because in this room,
I've made peace with what haunts me.
The light wouldn't chase them away.
It would only make them real.

Visitors

Things I've said to myself:
- ➤ "I don't know if I can do this."
- ➤ "Maybe tomorrow will be different."
- ➤ "What if I'm not enough?"
- ➤ "I'm tired of waiting."
- ➤ "I wish someone would understand."
- ➤ "I wish I could forget."
- ➤ "Maybe if I stay quiet, it'll pass."
- ➤ "Just one more day. Then I'll decide."
- ➤ "I shouldn't feel this way."
- ➤ "Maybe I deserve this."
- ➤ "I miss who I used to be."
- ➤ "No one would notice if I stopped trying."
- ➤ "I want to be seen without having to scream."
- ➤ "What's the point if it always ends the same?"
- ➤ "Maybe healing is just pretending better."
- ➤ "This isn't how I imagined growing up."

List No. 1

The clock snapped
its own spine.
The room flinched,
then forgot.
I live in the stillness,
where nothing grows,
and nothing fades.

Only the curtain stirs —
a slow, tired pulse,
dragging one scene into another.
A glass shattering mid-fall,
a goodbye
stitched into silence,
a laugh swallowed by dust.

I do not speak.
The air here punishes sound.
I only watch,
aching for a frame
where the breaking stops —
where the world does not end.

But the cloth keeps breathing,
pulling the ruins
back into shape.
I try to reach out,
try to pull a better scene through the cloth,
scrape a future from the folds.

The curtain trembles
the clock tightens its grip,
and the room offers me nothing.

The Curtain moves

I don't look in the mirror.
It holds my shape
like a body in a bag—
zippered with blood and flesh,
bulging with things I never said.

I feel my face slipping—
not enough to scream,
just enough to be wrong.
My nails peel at it,
as if guilt twitches underneath.

The mirror sees it all:
how my collarbones fold
like paper in the rain,
how my jaw creaks
when I try to smile— a hinge, rusted.

My eyes—
I didn't take them out,
but I turned them inward to see the rot.
They scream —
There are worms in my thoughts.

I don't look in the mirror because once,
I swear—
my reflection blinked first.
And I knew
it wasn't me anymore.

So, I keep the mirror covered—
in thin cloth, too thin.
And pass it quickly—
like skimming past a corpse
you once called by name.

Mirror eats first

The chair watches the world
more patiently than I ever could—
its wooden arms worn smooth
by time, by rain,
by the absence of yours.

I sit inside, eyes against the glass.
Dusk makes things dishonest.
There—
a silhouette leans into the chair's spine,
remembering the curve of your back.

I know it isn't you.
Too blurred at the edges,
like breath on a mirror.
But my heart—so gullible, so traitorous—
pulls the ghost closer anyway.

I wonder if the chair dreams too—
if it dreams in splinters and echoes,
of your hand tapping its armrest,
of your laugh falling softly
like a leaf no one caught.

Maybe it's the leaves I smoked.
The sky melts at the edges,
and the wind hums in voices
I almost remember.
I shouldn't trust my eyes, but I do.

But, the chair doesn't move.
Just leans into the silence,
as if it's tired
of pretending you're still coming back.

Ghost curves

[12th September, 2024 — 09:07 AM]

I hate to walk out of my room,
to walk down these halls
with eyes on nothing;
but torn shoes
creaking of mud, and
hands tracing the shape of my pockets,
as if they've forgotten
what to hold on to.

I do count the time in seconds,
and sometimes in hours,
in those hushes
that settle with each step.
Those weightless pauses
that scream in my ears
and taste like salt on my fingertips.

"Where are you going?"
"When will you come back?"
"Why are you still trying?"
"What are you holding onto?"
And yet, not a single word oozes
out of me—to myself.

But I listen to those screams,
not for answers—
just to be sure that
I'm not stuck,
I'm moving and
reaching somewhere,
so I can have a new pair of shoes
that won't make the floor go creak.

Pocket lines

[29th September, 2024 — 11:19 PM]

I lost the version of me
that understood silence —
the one who used to wait,
the one who sat in dark rooms
without mistaking every
shadow for a threat.

Now every quiet is a verdict.
The hum in the walls translates to run.
Breath holds its own breath.
Thoughts don't walk anymore—
they sprint and slip,
collide in hallways made of sand.

I forget the shape of sound,
like a name I never spoke out loud.
Buried it in the pause between
"What's wrong?" and
"Nothing."

I stitched noises into my ribs—
called it armour, called it prayer,
sometimes called it me.

Stitched to wires where
veins used to be,
and a flickering light behind my eyes
refuses to switch off.

But the silence keeps coming back,
sits on my chest
with the weight of all my unfinished sentences,
just to laugh at me and ask
if I've remembered how to listen.

I haven't.
But I lie and say I'm learning.
And the silence believes me—
or maybe
it just feel sorry.

Every quiet is a verdict

"You were never meant to be a perfect story — only an honest one."

[1ˢᵗ July, 2024 — 03:09 AM]

To you, in a borrowed skin.

I don't know when you'll find this. Maybe you'll forget you even wrote it. Maybe you'll stumble upon it during a cleaning spree, or on one of those days when you're just searching for something—anything—to make sense of the past.

Today was… hard. You know that kind of day? Where you wake up tired and somehow still manage to disappoint yourself before noon? Yeah. That. I sat on the floor for what must've been an hour. Just… sitting. Staring at nothing, thinking about nothing, and somehow still feeling everything all at once.

My chest aches and it's not even physical. I keep wondering if there's a limit to how tired a person can be without falling apart completely.

I sat down to write, thinking maybe it would help. But the words didn't come out right. Or they didn't come out at all. I just stared at the page, feeling stupid for trying. The pen kept slipping, and I think I was half-hoping it would do the writing for me. Spoiler: it didn't.

I feel hollow. Not sad, not angry—just empty. And scared.
I'm scared that this version of me might be the one that
stays. The one that never figures it out. The one who drifts
so far that no one notices when they disappear.
I don't know what I want from you. Maybe I just need to
know that someone—me, at least—will remember that
this happened. That it was real. That I wasn't just making it
up in my head.

I pressed a lavender between the pages. It felt important,
though I can't explain why. I think I just needed
something beautiful to survive this day. If it's still there
when you're reading this, I hope you'll understand what I
meant—even if I didn't.

Be softer than I could be.

With whatever love I have left,
Me.

Letter No. 3

[1ˢᵗ January, 2025 — 07:50 PM]

It wasn't deliberate—
just a peaceful evening at the windowsill
with dusty hands reaching at a book
I hadn't touched in years.
But that's how it works, isn't it?
You look for a pen
and end up holding your past.

The pages sighed
as I opened them—
old breath, old weight.
And there it was:
a folded piece of me,
creased at the corners,
thin as whispers from long ago.

The ink had surrendered—
bled out slowly,
until it became nothing
but ghost-bones of a letter.
I couldn't read the pain,
couldn't remember
how loud it once was.

I stared for a long time—
not at the tarnished paper,
but the bluish-purple petals:
a forget-me-not and hope,
squeezed flat in between
but unbroken,
wondering why I left it there.

Yet again, the room whispered to me,
and the coffee didn't grow cold.
It's softer—not because I forgot,
but because
I forgave myself.
The curtains still eager for a word,
I mumbled beneath my breath—Hi.

The room spoke second

[14th January, 2025 — 05:15 PM]

It fell without a reason
with no need to stitch the sky together.
Not asking if I was ready
it slipped into forgotten spaces—
between broken tiles,
under tired benches,
across long forgotten streets.

I could hear the noises dampening.
There were no apologies
in those puddles.
It did not try to fix anything.
Just touched everything —
soft and certain,
even the places left behind
were still worth reaching for.

Maybe,
I don't have to be the sun.
I do not have to be whole.
Maybe I can still fall —
quiet, unnoticed,
and still be enough.

I stood still,
letting the water gather at my feet,
letting the dust lift away
without asking why it was there.
The rain — it knew me,
even when I didn't know
how to ask for it.

The rain knew me

[7th February, 2025 — 10:20 PM]

This morning, the red thread pulled itself free—
loose, soft, unwounded.
It wasn't tight anymore.
It didn't cling to my wrist,
didn't choke the air around me
with its constant reminder.

I let it fall, watched it rest,
coiled in the corner of the room like a memory
I no longer needed to keep.
I reached for it then,
not out of obligation but out of curiosity.
What if this thread was never meant to
bind me?

I followed it—
and it led me to places
I hadn't yet dreamed,
through doors I'd locked in my mind
before I even knew how to open them.
The thread didn't pull at my skin anymore,
it danced ahead of me like
an invitation to a future
I thought I couldn't reach.

I tugged at it gently, and with each pull,
the world unfolded a little wider.
The fabric of my days loosened,
stretched into shapes
I could walk through,
shapes that felt like possibility instead of a cage.

I stopped wearing long sleeves,
and let my skin feel the warmth of sunlight
that had always been there.

It didn't pull me into the past anymore,
but forward, into the space where
I was waiting for me.
Smiling, arms open wide,
ready to show me how to live
without the weight of the world
pressing against my chest.

It wasn't a trap but a guide back home.

The red path

[20th March, 2025 — 01:15 PM]

I.   The First Floor:

It was made of paper,
thin walls built from my hands—
I remember bending
over in the backyard,
pretending the small tree was a door,
pressing my ear to the bark
like I could hear
the heartbeat of the house inside.

The rooms were filled with laughter
that sounded like rain,
light flickering through gaps in the roof
where sunlight never stopped
trying to come in.

I carried it in my chest,
a fragile thing with spaces
between the beams,
a place where nothing ever broke,
and the cracks were only shadows.

71

II.   The Second Floor:

The walls grew heavier.
I began to notice the weight
of the stairs,
the way my knees shook
under the load.

The house creaked in the dark.
It whispered things
I couldn't understand—
the kind of words you find
in the forgotten corners of your mind.

I tried to fill the rooms
with things I didn't need—
books that never made sense,
pictures I couldn't recognize,
stories that didn't belong to me.

And yet, I stayed.
I carried the house like a burden,
the space between the walls
growing colder every day.

III.   The Third Floor:

I knocked against the windows,
but the light never came.
The house began to lean,
one side pressing lower than the other.
I could feel it in my bones,
the weight of everything that had been left unsaid.

I carried the empty rooms—
cracked mirrors, shattered windows,
furniture that had lost its purpose.
The door to the attic was locked,
but I could feel the dust and silence creeping down
from above.

In the evenings,
I'd sit by the door,
waiting for someone to come—
to fix the broken parts of the house,
to rearrange the rooms
and make it feel like home again.

But no one came.
I carried the house alone.

IV.   The Fourth Floor:

Time passed like soft
footsteps on the stairs.
The weight didn't change,
but I did.

The cracks in the walls softened,
and the rooms became —
quieter.

I let the dust settle,
moved the furniture into
new spaces, and
for the first time,
I noticed the light coming
through the windows again.

It wasn't bright or loud.
But it was there,
quietly filling the spaces
that had once been
empty.

V.   The Fifth Floor:

And now,
I stand at the door,
the house still on my back,
but I no longer carry it alone.
The rooms are familiar,
but I don't need to live in them anymore.
I've learned how to leave.

I walk out.
I set the house down.
The ground feels different—
softer than I imagined.
And the sky above me
seems so much bigger now.

The house will always be with me,
but it no longer needs to be carried.
It just exists,
a place of memories,
of things left behind.

The House

There's more in my room now,
Not just a bed, a mirror, and a shelf.
The space feels fuller—
light reaches the corners,
a chair, a table cluttered with things
that makes it feel like mine.
The phantom book is still here,
but it's speaking now,
whispering words
I can understand now.

I open it slowly,
its pages worn smooth.
No longer do they catch fire,
they unfold gently,
like memories flying
softly off my chest one by one.
The moths are still there,
resting on the pages,
whispering secrets.
I once thought they were warnings.
The potatoes, the scribbles,
the random tears—
each piece of the puzzle fits.

The shelf feels different now,
not just a place to hold things,
but a place for memories, possibilities,
futures that stir softly, like a breeze in this room.

Each page, each scribble,
has a story I've forgotten I needed to hear.
Some are faint echoes of things
I thought were lost, while others are fresh—
a thread pulled from tomorrow,
writing out my name.
The room isn't empty anymore, and neither am I.
The book, the shelf, the chair, the mirror—
They are me.
Pieces of me, I couldn't reach or grasp
They were waiting for me.

Now, I know—
The book isn't just watching over me.
It's writing me into being,
one page at a time.

The library for all

The bench
still leans a little to the left,
the paint chipped at the armrest
where I used to draw circles
with my thumb
while waiting for you
to finish your stories.

The tree above remembers
how to bloom,
careless pinks and
yellows stretching like a yawn—
as if the sky itself is trying again,
softly, hesitantly
but trying.

There's no trace
of you on the bench,
but the seat doesn't feel entirely empty.
I sit the way I always did:
one leg tucked under,
hands quiet,
eyes on the path that bends away.

You don't sit beside me anymore.
But the wind doesn't mind.
It plays with the edge of my scarf,
nudges fallen petals onto my lap—
like it knows
I needed something gentle today.
A child runs past, laughter trailing
like wind-bells.
I smile at the echo.

April is kinder this time.
It doesn't ask questions.
It only lets me sit—
until I stop glancing at the path,
and begin watching the sky instead.

An empty bench in April

[15th May, 2025 — 11:50 PM]

This is for the friend
who sat beside me on cracked cement
while I cried about nothing I could name—
offering only her shadow
and the warmth of her silence.

For the old ceiling fan
that whispered in slow, sleepy circles
on nights when the world felt too loud,
never fixing anything,
but never leaving either.

For the night lamp,
who blinked patiently
through every scribbled page and tear,
its dim glow never judging
my unfinished thoughts.

To the tea mug
that held warmth longer than most people,
and to the scarf
that caught more of my sadness
than I ever let out loud.

To the strangers who passed me
on empty roads
and smiled anyway,
as if saying, "I see you,"
without asking to know why.

To the diary that listened,
page after page,
without advice, without cure,
only space.

And to the version of me
who stayed—
even when I didn't want to.

Thank you for never rushing me.
For knowing that some healing
doesn't speak.
It simply sits beside you
until you're ready to look up.

The ones who stayed

[5th June, 2025 — 07:20 AM]

It used to land heavy
like a boulder
dropped in a quiet room,
each syllable;
sharp and uncertain
echoing through places
I once tried to shrink
and disappear.

For years I flinched,
when people said it aloud
as if they were seeking
a part of me
I hadn't made peace with,
and it wasn't meant
to be seen by someone else.

But lately I say it differently
not loud but gentler-
when I'm folding my clothes
or looking at the mirror
I whisper those syllables
as if I'm introducing
me to myself.

It no longer feels borrowed or a burden.
My name-
It's just a word,
and yet somehow it hums
asking me to no longer hide,
urging me to smile and say
"Hi".

A quiet 'Hi'

[8th June, 2025 — 11:25 PM]

To you, with lighter hands,

There was a letter I never sent. I wrote it, folded it, and kept it close. I thought there would be a better time, a better version of myself, a better way to say everything.

She waited without knowing she was waiting. And I stayed silent, thinking the feeling itself would be enough. Thinking maybe people could hear the things you don't say out loud.

I'm sorry for that.
For thinking silence was safer than trying and failing. For letting the fear of saying it wrong become worse than saying nothing at all. She deserved the letter — the one that said thank you, and I'm here, and I see you. She deserved the clumsy words, the messy ink and the heart that couldn't quite get it right but wanted to.

I owed her more courage than I had. And maybe I still do.

But I owe you, too —
I owe you the forgiveness of small mistakes, the gentleness of knowing that sometimes even love can come late. You didn't mean to be careless. You didn't mean to let the moment pass by unopened.

84

And the fact that you still think about it now —
that you still wish you had done better —
means you are already becoming someone who will.
Some letters don't reach the people they were meant for.
But maybe they find their way back to you instead, quietly
teaching you how to be softer, how to be braver, next
time.

It's not too late. It was never too late.

A softer - clumsier you, yet again under the sunlight.
Me.

Letter No. 4

[9th June, 2025 — 00:10 AM]

The sky —
still breathes in saffron,
like the day we stitched our promises
beneath trembling leaves.
The trees hum with yesterday,
their roots tangled in our
old dreams.

I remember—
two foolish kids, chasing comets,
believing the half-moon could sew us forever.
I ran so hard, I forgot I had feet.
I reached so far, I forgot I had hands.
But somewhere among the stars,
I lost myself.

Today,
I tilt my face toward the sun —
no longer a ghost,
no longer a shadow.
I gather the dust off my bones.
Let the golden hours bleed into my cracks.
And let the sky write new promises
across my shoulders.

I owe the sun an apology:
For the times I ran alone,
For years I mistook reflection for light.
Forgive me —
for loving with closed fists,
for calling sorrow by the name of devotion.
Today, I offer my open palms.

And if someday,
your laughter slips back into the breeze,
and you stand again beneath this saffron sky,
I'll meet you —
not with prayers stitched into my skin,
but with my whole heart burning.

No more chasing comets.
No more seeking the missing halves.
Only light —
only home.

Promise..?

"Even wilted petals remember the sun"

[10th July, 2025 — 10:10 AM]

I did wish for a warmer winter,
Having a woollen blanket
over my shoulders, not soaked.
Instead of smothering flames underneath,
maybe a baby fire, kindling down my toes.

"Go back home."

The words grumbled out of my coffee mug.
Maybe she, too, recognizes the sweater
from years ago, that once had her close.
Trying to smudge away the fog,
and wobbling his way up to my window;
he grumbles back:

"You should come out often."
"Right now? In the middle of the night..."

It was stupid of me to ask.
Those eyes were
about to run around in shorts,
with cheeks blushing and cracking up.

Maybe a little dance around a bonfire, or
crawling down to play hide and...
"Hide and seek. Will you join me? I'll be 'it'."
"No!" A blunt response.

Asking me not to burn myself up,
he scraped around his pockets.
A pinch of salt,
a handful of lime, and
some dirt along with it.

But had I ever seen something as free
as those charcoal fingers?

"Have this potato. It's ours anyways!"

Salt, lime and dirt

A note on time

These pages carry dates, some real, some imagined.
Like thoughts scribbled in the margins of days not yet
lived.
They do not follow time –
They follow feelings.

Some entries are from afternoons that never came.
Some are letters to a future self, still learning how to speak.
If you find a date that hasn't happened yet, perhaps it's
because hope writes ahead of calendar.

About the author

Rajesh Kumar Gouda writes poetry born from quiet reflection and the search for meaning in life's smallest moments. With a deep interest in exploring themes of self-discovery, isolation, and hope, his words often speak to those who find solace in the unsaid.

Through poetry, he captures the delicate balance between longing and growth, offering a voice to those who navigate the subtle spaces between being lost and found. Each poem is an invitation to step into a world of quiet introspection and soft revelation.

Connect with the author:
Instagram: @rajeshkr.gouda
Email: rajeshgouda107@gmail.com

"I didn't arrive where I thought I would,
But I stayed—and that changed everything."